Presented to:

_____

Presented by:

_____

On this date:

_____

PETE, FEET, AND FISH TO EAT

BY PHIL A. SMOUSE

A Barbour Book

Fantastic! Amazing! They'll never believe it.
It's such a surprise, I can hardly conceive it.

An hour ago, I was locked in a cell
full of jeeper creep-peepers and dust-musty smells.
I was chained to the wall. I was chained to the door.
I was chained to the lamp and the chair and the floor!

Then a voice, still and small, like a beautiful light,
whispered, "Peter, look up!" and to my great delight...

My chains were all broken. I was up on my feet.
I was out of that prison and back on the street!

Now, as you might have guessed, I was rather excited
to be so completely removed and uprighted.
I flew down the alley. I kicked up the dust.
I raced through the darkness, full speed ahead plus...

Finish the story? Get on with it? Do it?!
All right, just sit tight, and I'll get around *TO* it!

"Start at the start." That's what Mom used to say.
There was just no forgetting that one certain day...
We were washing our nets. We'd been fishing all night,
and my brother and I had a terrible fight.

"It's a beautiful fish, I would tend to agree,
and the only one singular fish that I see!
After thirty-one hours of huffing and sweating,
there's one teeny, tiny, small thing you're forgetting.

One trivial, trifling, petty, slim thought:

IN A DAY AND A HALF,
THIS IS ALL THAT
WE'VE CAUGHT!"

I was frothing and foaming, steaming and stewing, yes, gritting and grinding and chafing and chewing!

I was so caught away in my little black cloud that I never did notice the wonderful crowd of a hundred, or maybe a thousand or more, who squash-squeezed and crunch-crowded their way to the shore.

"Teach us, O Lord!" I heard them all shout
as they hustled and bustled and rustled about.

And there went my brother. He was shouting it, too.
Why, the place had turned into
some kind of a zoo!

Well, *that's* when it happened.
He came up to *me*,
this man they were eyeing
and trying to see.

He stepped into my boat, and He asked for a lift;
so I hoisted the sail, and I set her adrift.

"Cast out your nets," He proclaimed, "if you wish,
and you'll find that they're filled full to bursting with fish."

"Whatever you say...." (This should really be good!)
We'll probably snag a few pieces of wood,
or maybe some cans or a shoe or a boot
or a water-logged wallet. Now *that* would be cute!

What happened next was a little bit shocking.
It sent my head spinning. It set my knees knocking!

Fish by the tens and the hundreds of dozens—
fish uncles and aunts, nephews, nieces, and cousins—
were cramming my nets. And before I could blink,
my poor boat was so full that it started to sink.

"Oh, Lord!" I cried out as I fell at His feet
and proceeded to whimper and sniffle and bleat.

"Go away from me. Please, please, just leave me alone!
I'm the worst kind of horrible man ever known."

But HE didn't care. It was perfectly fine.
I could tell as His eyes looked down deep into mine.
And right then and there, in that boat, on that day,
Jesus wiped all my badness and sadness away.

(But if you think *that's* something, then listen to this,
because *this* will be something you won't want to miss....)

I remember that night us guys were recollecting
as we laughed and we hugged, all the while interjecting.
But amid the munching and crunching and chewing,
I noticed this strange thing that Jesus was doing.

He'd taken a bowl and a towel and a seat,
and proceeded to wash
every one of our feet.
Our *feet,* of all things!
Yes, He sat there
among us. He plucked
every toe-jam and flushed
every fungus!

"Not *my* feet, Lord! No, they are not for You to clean!"
(Isn't there something *wrong* with this scene?)
"I'm certain there's something *important* to do
For someone who's someone like someone like You...."

Well, He looked at that bowl, and I knew in a minute
He wanted my two big, fat feet to be in it!

"All right, then," I blathered, "well, how about this...

I'll go get a sponge and a mop and a hose,
and we'll scrubble and bubble
        my knees and my nose.
Then we'll wish-wash my eyebrows
and swish-swash my hips.
We'll polish my forehead
and lather my lips!"

"Calm down. Pull the plug,
Peter. Put it on ice!
Can't you see that I'm trying
to do something nice?"

"Just relax," Jesus whispered, "and listen up well,
because now *I'm* the one with a story to tell!"

The story He told us was shocking and frightening.

Our eyes were bug-bulging, our stomachs twist-tightening.

He said He'd be battered, bruised, beaten and *killed*;
but the Word of the Lord would at last be fulfilled!
Then, to top it all off, He said I
would deny
that I ever did know
Him! "Oh, no, Lord!" I cried.

"Before the cock crows, you'll
deny Me three times."
How I wished I could
get those words out of my mind.

As they dragged Him away,
we were yelling and screaming.
This can't be for real.
I just have to be dreaming!

"Hey, you with the beard and the big bony knees,
come on over here, I'd like to talk to you, please!
I know your face, and I know it quite well.
You were with Him, that Jesus. I know. I can tell!"

"Mind your own business! Get out of my sight!
I don't know Him, OR YOU, so just drop it, all right?"

"We know you were there,
you could hardly be missed."
"You're mistaken!" I bellowed
and boiled and hissed.
"Yes, I saw him, too.
There can't be any doubt!"
an old, gravelly-gray,
dusty voice gurgled out.

"I DON'T KNOW THE MAN! Would you all just be QUIET!
Please, leave me alone. Be still, calm down, come on now, let's try it!"

Yes, I denied Him, and they crucified Him.
I watched as they did it. I stood right beside Him.
But there's something I think that you really should know.
It's something He told me a long time ago...

"Peter," He said, "I AM LOVE, and you'll find
that I'm ever so patient and wonderfully kind.
I'm NOT keeping a list. I'm NOT checking it twice.
No, TIIAT would be naughty and not at all nice."

Oh, I've messed it up now. Lord, I've messed it up then.
Yes, I've messed it up over and over again.
Dear Lord Jesus, forgive me. Please bring me back home.
I'm the worst kind of horrible man ever known.

The past is forgotten. Erased! Oh, it's true.
He did it for me. He *WILL* do it for you!